I0058390

ISS.

Dediu Newsletter

Author: Michael M. Dediu

Monthly news, reviews, comments and suggestions for a better and wiser world

Vol. 2, Nr. 12 (24), 6 November 2018

DERC Publishing House

Tewksbury (Boston), Massachusetts, U. S. A.

For subscriptions please use the contact form at www.derc.com

Published and printed in the
United States of America
On the Great Seal of the United States are included:
E Pluribus Unum (Out of many, one)
Annuit Coeptis (He has approved of the undertakings)
Novus Ordo Seclorum (New order of the ages)

Dediu, Michael M.

Dediu Newsletter Vol 2, Number 12 (24), 6 November 2018
Monthly reviews, comments and suggestions for a better and wiser world

ISSN 2475-2061
ISBN 978-1-939757-78-4

Preface

October 2018 was full of events, some pleasant, some not, which reminds us to keep working to prevent and eliminate those unpleasant events.

There are many good news from research in science, medicine, technology, and other areas: a new robot could revive an abandoned prostatectomy procedure, artificial intelligence is not only helping now and for the foreseeable future, but it's also going to have a much stronger presence in medical technology as time goes on, Virgin Galactic is in a closely-fought commercial space race with Jeff Bezos's Blue Origin, a company has launched the 'Relay robot,' a new fully autonomous service robot designed to optimize labor productivity in hospital lab environments.

In this 12th newsletter of the second volume, the 24th in total, we included the most relevant news, in a balanced approach, usually directly from the source, to help the general public better understand the realities around us. We included also several nice photos - I thank my wife for her photo assistance. Being well and correctly informed is a sine qua non requirement for everybody, in order to make the right decisions for the future.

Enjoy this newsletter and be optimist!

Michael M. Dediu, Ph. D.

Tewksbury (Boston), U. S. A., 6 November 2018

USA, Chicago, founded in 1837: London Guarantee Building (1923, 22 floors, 96 m), on North Michigan Avenue.

Table of Contents

Canada, Niagara Falls: Niagara SkyWheel in Dinosaur Park and Miniature Golf, near Clifton Hill and Oneida Lane, 1.5 km north of the Horseshoe Falls on Niagara River.

United States of America

(Population 324.4 M, rank 3, growth 0.7%. Free: 89 of 100).
Reports: In the U.S., where federally marijuana is not legal, some states are moving in the opposite direction.

Friday, 28 September 2018. Reports: Facebook said that an attack on its computer network made the personal information of nearly 50 millions of users vulnerable. With personal information, criminals can sell it on the criminals' web, takeover or open new accounts, file fake tax returns and more.
People ask for the arrest of cybercriminals.

Reports: Americans deserve a real conversation about the prodigious rate at which the federal government has grown at the expense of taxpayers. Recounting the details of what Congress passed last week of September would be routine, if it weren't so disappointing. Ahead of a forever-looming government shutdown at the end of the month, Congress sent the president a historically large spending package. Passed by a margin of 300 (361 to 61), the measure clocks in at $854 B in spending, and combines with prior measures to add up to nearly $1 trillion. It is obvious that the DC establishment abuses the legislative process to shield themselves from the will of the voters.

Reports: The latest report on the "Economic Freedom of the World," published last week by Canada's Fraser Institute and the Cato Institute, and using data up through 2016. "The foundations of economic freedom are personal choice, voluntary exchange, and open markets," write the authors — though there's rather a lot more behind the numbers, as you might expect.
All of this should be important to Americans because the U.S. has been sliding in the rankings for many, many years. The 2012 report mourned that "[f]rom 1980 to 2000, the United States was generally rated the third freest economy in the world, ranking behind only Hong Kong and Singapore," but that it "has experienced a substantial decline in economic freedom during the past decade."

Crypto-mining infections are growing very much this year. Cybercriminals are hijacking people's network processing power and are stealing workstation and server resources. They are using various types of malware trying to stay under the radar.

In February 2018, it was confirmed that the cybercriminals committed the largest DDoS attack ever at an unprecedented level of 1.7 Tbps.

People are asking the authorities to arrest the cybercriminals.

Reports: The U.S. government closed out the 2018 fiscal year $779 B in the red as expenses rose on a growing national debt. The deficit was also larger than any year since 2012, when it topped $1T. Adding to debt servicing costs, the Federal Reserve is raising interest rates roughly once per quarter in the face of a hot labor market, and some signs of inflation.

Reports: according to a new 2018 CEO and Executive Compensation Report: Median CEO pay for 2017 was $350,622, with no increase year over year. That's 6.7 times the median income for all U.S. workers ($52,331).

Reports: The United States is back on top as the most competitive country in the world, regaining the No. 1 spot for the first time since 2008, in an index produced by the World Economic Forum.

Reports: Changes in Congress: from fair play to power plays. The United States Congress has been described as dysfunctional, gridlocked, polarized, hyper-partisan, chaotic, and do-nothing. There is an institutional dynamic behind Congress's devolution from a respected legislative institution, to a body plagued by a win-at-any-cost mentality, and by perpetual campaigning. In the past decade, under both Republican and Democratic majorities, both parties have gamed what the founders intended would be an impartial set of legislative rules, into a system that advantages majorities and marginalizes minorities. There is a clear legislative leaders' inability to find substantive policy solutions that are in the national interest.

Reports: Many say that the national debt is the greatest existential threat to the United States today. It is crucial for Congress to get serious about reining in the reckless government spending that puts America's future at risk.

The previous administration added $245 B in regulatory costs in its first 21 months.

What the data reveal is that the 1,409 individuals, the top 0.001%, pay 3% of individual income taxes. The top 1% pay 37.3% of individual income taxes. The top 3% pay a full 51% of individual taxes. The top 3% of the individual income earners earn 29% of all adjusted gross income, but already pay 51% of all individual income taxes. By contrast, the bottom 97% of taxpayers earn 71% of adjusted gross income and pay 49% of individual income taxes.

Reports: ACT scores show drop in college readiness, especially in mathematics.

Law school grads reach a new low on Massachusetts bar exam.

Reports: Of the roughly 30 millions of business in the U.S., fewer than 6,000 are publicly traded and only the largest 8.3% of these public companies make it into the S&P 500. Yet, most media outlets repeat the $12.1 M median annual pay package static for these 500 highest paid CEOs, leading to many mistaken assumptions about CEO pay of the remaining 30 M CEOs.

Reports: The U.S. unsecured personal loan market is growing at 20% annually, and has surpassed $125 B in balances.

30 October 2018. Reports: The U.S. Treasury Department expects to issue $425 B in debt this quarter, bringing government borrowing this year to $1.34 T, more than double from 2017.

30 October 2018. Reports: A week away from the midterm elections, the Pentagon is sending 5,200 troops to the Mexican border to stop Central American migrants traveling north in two caravans from entering the U.S. The number of soldiers is more than double the 2,000 who are fighting in Syria.

Reports: Students from low-income neighborhoods, who attended a high-achieving school, were less likely to abuse marijuana, than those who weren't admitted. By 11th grade, the risk of misusing the drug was cut by half in boys at top-performing schools.
– University of California, Los Angeles (UCLA), Health Sciences

Puerto Rico: (Population 3.6 M, rank 134, decrease 0.1%; an unincorporated territory of the United States, located in the northeast Caribbean Sea, 1,600 km southeast of Miami, Florida.).

United Nations.   There are 195 officially recognized countries. Around 44,000 people work for the United Nations. There is a wide range of jobs: Researchers, IT-specialists, lawyers, experts on finance and administration, or translators work at the New York headquarters, at the official locations, or at specialized agencies. More than half of the UN's workforce is employed in the field, in projects of humanitarian aid, or on peace missions.

The International Court of Justice is the highest United Nations court. While the World Court's rulings are binding, it has no power to enforce them, and the US. and Iran are both among a handful of countries that have ignored its decisions.

Reports: The International Court of Justice has ordered the U.S. to lift sanctions on humanitarian goods for Iran, although the U.S. administration made clear the decision wouldn't change anything, and pulled out of the 1955 Treaty of Amity (on which the lawsuit was based). The agreement was signed by President Dwight D. Eisenhower, 65, (14 Oct 1890 – 28 March 1969, aged 78.4, President 20 Jan 1953 – 20 Jan 1961), and the Shah of Iran Mohammad Reza Pahlavi, 36, (26 Oct 1919, Tehran, Iran – 27 July 1980, Cairo, Egypt, aged 60.7, shah for 38 years: 1941 - 1979), long before Iran's 1979 Islamic Revolution (the U.S. President was Jimmy Carter, 55, (1 Oct 1924, now 94 years old, President 20 Jan 1977 – 20 Jan 1981), the shah was 60 and left to Egypt) that turned the two countries into arch enemies.

Chicago, 1837: from the Skydeck (floor 103, 412 m) of Willis Tower (1973, 108 floors, 527 m) a view of the south-east part of Chicago, with Lake Michigan (left up).

China, Japan, and neighbors

China: (Population 1.4 B, rank 1, growth 0.4%. Freedom House reports for 2018: Not Free (15 of 100)). Reports: It seems that China's new laser satellite will be able to detect and track deep-diving submerged submarines.

History: In 2010, the jailed Chinese human rights activist Liu Xiaobo won the Nobel Peace Prize. He died of cancer in 2017.

5 October 2018. Reports: China responded overnight to U.S. Vice President Mike Pence, after Washington's Nr. 2 accused China of "malign" efforts to undermine the U.S. elections process, and "reckless" military actions in the South China Sea. "This is nothing but speaking on hearsay evidence, confusing right and wrong, and creating something out of thin air," according to China's foreign ministry. Pence also took aim at Google's Project Dragonfly, saying it would accelerate Chinese censorship efforts.

5 October 2018. Reports: There is a report that alleged Chinese spy chips were discovered in data center equipment used by Amazon and Apple. The tech giants have denied the allegations by Bloomberg Businessweek, which said the hack reached almost 30 U.S. companies and compromised America's technology supply chain.

Reports: China exported more in September, producing a record trade surplus of $34.13 B with the U.S. that could intensify an already heated trade dispute. The figure further surged to $225.79 B over the January-September period.

Reports: The total censorship era is here, and some Chinese journalists reflect on their experiences. Also, the Chinese government works to censor debate in western democracies.

16 October 2018. Xinhua. Chinese President Xi Jinping on Monday, 15 Oct, called for a stronger sense of mission for deeper military-civilian integration.
Xi, also general secretary of the Communist Party of China (CPC) Central Committee and chairman of the Central Military Commission, made the remarks while presiding over the second session of the Central Commission for Integrated Military and Civilian Development, which he also heads.

He asked for a stronger hold on the implementation of the integration, strengthened role of rule of law, deeper reform of system, and further coordinated innovation in science and technology. The meeting deliberated and passed a guideline on strengthening the development of rule of law in integrated military and civilian development.

Wang Huning and Han Zheng, both members of the Standing Committee of the Political Bureau of the CPC Central Committee and deputy heads of the Central Commission for Integrated Military and Civilian Development, also attended the meeting.

Attendees of the meeting stressed the implementation of the guideline, the improvement of the legal system and further legislation on military-civilian integration, in order to ensure the legislation covers all major areas.

The system and mechanism for the integration should be enhanced to make sure that issues are mulled over, decisions are made and tasks are handled within the ranges of law.

A fairer market environment must be built to push forward competitive procurement, to guide state-owned military industrial enterprises to open up in an orderly manner, and to increase the ratio of civilian and private enterprises that take part in such competition, it was agreed at the meeting.

Noting that building major strategic projects is an effective way to promote sci-tech innovation, attendees of the meeting called for making breakthroughs in key and core technologies. Building projects should play a leading role in the process, while advantages and strength should be concentrated and coordinated to make breakthroughs as soon as possible, according to the meeting.

The participants also called for the strengthening of the centralized and unified leadership of the CPC Central Committee, giving full play to the political advantage of the system of socialism with Chinese characteristics capable of pooling all necessary resources to solve major problems, coordinating major relevant projects and plans, as well as mobilizing necessary human, financial and material resources. Party committees and governments at all levels should take it as a major political responsibility to implement the military-civilian integration, be brave to reform and innovate and work hard to make new progress in deeper development of military-civilian integration, according to the meeting.

Reports: The big hack: how China used a tiny chip to infiltrate U.S. companies and computer servers.

Reports: China is developing lidar-based satellite for detection of deep-diving submarine forces.

Reports: China's holdings of U.S. Treasuries fell for a third consecutive month in August, dropping $6 B to $1.165 T. Beijing's sale of Treasuries is viewed as a response to the ongoing trade war, especially after China's ambassador to the U.S. signaled in March his country could scale back purchases of the debt to retaliate against tariffs.

18 October 2018. In Russia, Vladimir Putin had a meeting with Yang Jiechi, member of the Political Bureau of the CPC Central Committee and Director of the Office of the Foreign Affairs Commission. Vladimir Putin noted that Russia will continue to work towards the implementation of the agreements reached during Chinese President Xi Jinping's visit to Vladivostok to attend the Eastern Economic Forum, and praised the level of development in the two countries' relations. The President asked Yang Jiechi to give his best regards to President Xi.

22 October 2018. Reports: President Xi vowed "unwavering" support for non-state firms over the weekend, while the country's stock exchanges committed to help manage share-pledge risks, and the government released a plan to cut personal income taxes.

22 October 2018. Xinhua. President Xi Jinping has encouraged private entrepreneurs to have firm confidence in development, and work in a down-to-earth way to develop their businesses. Xi, also general secretary of the Communist Party of China (CPC) Central Committee, and chairman of the Central Military Commission, made the remarks in a letter on Saturday, 21 Oct, in response to some private entrepreneurs having been awarded for their contributions in a poverty relief campaign.

In his letter, Xi spoke highly of the private entrepreneurs' devotion to the cause of fighting poverty.

"I'm delighted to see an increasing number of private entrepreneurs actively shouldering social responsibilities, eagerly devoting themselves to the arduous battle to eradicate poverty, and helping many impoverished people to live a better life," Xi said.

Over 60,000 private enterprises have taken part in the poverty relief campaign, named "10,000 enterprises assisting 10,000 villages," since it started in October 2015, with 100 of them being awarded earlier this month. The awarded private entrepreneurs recently sent Xi a letter, reporting the experiences of participating in the campaign, and expressing their determination to further contribute to poverty eradication.

In the responding letter, Xi said that private enterprises had been thriving, and the private economy had been growing in size and strength in the reform and opening-up drive over the past 40 years.

The private economy plays a key role in promoting steady growth, innovation and employment, as well as improving people's wellbeing, and has become an important driving force for social and economic development, he said.

The private economy's historic contributions are indelible, and its position and functions should not be doubted, Xi said. "Any word or act to deny or weaken the private economy is wrong."

Supporting the development of private enterprises has been a consistent principle of the CPC Central Committee, which will be unwaveringly implemented, he stressed.

"I hope that private entrepreneurs will grasp the trend of the era, have firm confidence in development, innovate and create without being distracted, and work in a down-to-earth way in developing their businesses, to jointly create a better tomorrow for the private economy, and make greater contributions to realizing the Chinese Dream of national rejuvenation," Xi said.

23 October 2018. Xinhua: Chinese President Xi Jinping announced the opening of the Hong Kong-Zhuhai-Macao Bridge at a launch ceremony in the city of Zhuhai, Guangdong Province, on Tuesday, 23 Oct, morning.

On behalf of the Communist Party of China (CPC) Central Committee, Xi, also general secretary of the CPC Central Committee and chairman of the Central Military Commission, expressed sincere thanks and warm greetings to those who participated in the design, building, and management of the bridge.

Han Zheng, vice premier and member of the Standing Committee of the Political Bureau of the CPC Central Committee, addressed the opening ceremony, which was held at a hall of the Zhuhai Port.

The 55-km bridge, situated in the waters of Lingdingyang of Pearl River Estuary, connects the Hong Kong Special Administrative Region (SAR), Zhuhai and the Macao SAR. The bridge is the first of its kind for Guangdong, Hong Kong, and Macao, to jointly build a supergiant sea-crossing traffic project under the principle of "one country, two systems."

At 9:30 a.m., Xi was greeted at the hall by a standing ovation amid joyful music. After watching a video on the building of the bridge, Li Xi, member of the Political Bureau of the CPC Central Committee and secretary of the CPC Guangdong Provincial Committee, Carrie Lam, chief executive of the Hong Kong SAR, Chui Sai On, chief executive of the Macao SAR, and Han Zheng delivered speeches respectively.

At about 10 a.m., Xi walked up to the podium and announced the opening of the bridge. After the ceremony, Xi rode in a vehicle to tour and inspect the bridge.

During the inspection, Xi ascended on a platform to overlook the bridge at the east artificial island, which is a key part of the bridge.

The bridge is a national project. "You participated in the design, building, and maintenance of the bridge, gave full play to your talents and wisdom, and accomplished the tasks with good quality and quantity," Xi said, adding that he is proud of such achievements.

Praising builders of the bridge for breaking a number of world records, Xi said they demonstrate the nation's spirit of striving to overcome any difficulties, the national strength, the innovative ability, and the aspiration to be the world's best.

"With the bridge, we have further enhanced our confidence in the path, theory, system, and culture of socialism with Chinese characteristics," Xi said.

The bridge should not only be structurally sound but also well managed, in a bid to contribute to the development of the Guangdong-Hong Kong-Macao Greater Bay Area, he said.

The bridge will help improve personnel and trade exchanges among Guangdong, Hong Kong, and Macao, benefit the development of the area, and enhance the comprehensive competitiveness of the Pearl River Delta, Han said.

He stressed that the bridge is important for supporting Hong Kong and Macao in integrating their own development into the overall development of the country, and fully advancing mutually beneficial cooperation among the mainland, Hong Kong, and Macao.

The construction of the bridge began on Dec. 15, 2009, and its main structure was completed on July 7, 2017.

The bridge will officially open to traffic at 9 a.m. on Oct. 24.

25 October 2018. Xinhua: President Xi Jinping has called for building the country's pilot free trade zones (FTZs) toward new heights of reform and opening-up in the new era. Xi, also general secretary of the Communist Party of China (CPC) Central Committee and chairman of the Central Military Commission, made the remarks in an instruction on the development of pilot FTZs.

The development of pilot FTZs is a strategic measure by the CPC Central Committee in advancing reform and opening-up in the new era, and has become a milestone in the course, Xi said.

Five years of enterprising and pioneering work in the country's pilot FTZs has seen major progress and breakthroughs, offering the nation copious advances in institutional explorations, Xi said.

Xi also urged more efforts in advancing the development of pilot FTZs to generate more replicable institutional innovation, to make greater contributions in achieving China's two centenary goals, and national rejuvenation.

26 October 2018. Xinhua: Chinese President Xi Jinping has called for greater resolve and stronger measures in deepening China's reform and opening-up in the new era.

Xi, also general secretary of the Communist Party of China (CPC) Central Committee and chairman of the Central Military Commission, made the remarks during his inspection tour of southern Guangdong Province from Monday, 22 Oct, to Thursday, 25 Oct. "The international and domestic environment has undergone extensive and profound changes in the new era, presenting the reform and opening-up with new circumstances, tasks and challenges," Xi said. "To seize opportunities and counter challenges, the key is upholding the banner of reform and opening-up in the new era, and continuously deepen reform and expand opening-up in a comprehensive way, " he said. Xi visited places including Zhuhai, Qingyuan, Shenzhen and Guangzhou, where he learned about the work on applying the guiding principles of the CPC's 19th National Congress, deepening reform and opening up, as well as advancing high-quality economic development. On Monday afternoon, Xi visited an industrial park for traditional Chinese medicine (TCM) in the Hengqin New area in Zhuhai, a pioneer project developed under a cooperation agreement between Guangdong and Macao.

Xi called for more efforts in exploring the essence of TCM and better collaboration between enterprises, universities and research institutes to advance the industrialization, modernization and globalization of TCM.

He also urged stronger policy support for deepening and expanding cooperation between Hengqin and Macao in developing emerging industries to inject more vitality into Macao's economy.

Later in the afternoon, Xi visited home appliances maker Gree Electric Appliances, inspecting its independent core technology research and development department, and holding talks with research staff in a national key laboratory on energy efficiency of air-conditioning products.

"The real economy is the foundation of a country's economy and source of wealth. Advanced manufacturing is one key area of the real economy and the economic development cannot be separated from the real economy at any time," he said.

Independent innovation is the only way towards scaling world heights in science and technology, and all enterprises should make arduous efforts towards this direction, he said.

"Enterprises should have the aspirations and guts to accelerate enhancing the capability of independent innovation, strive to achieve the independent control of key core technologies and hold firmly the initiative of innovative development in our own hands," he said.

On Tuesday afternoon, Xi inspected an e-commerce industrial park in the city of Qingyuan in central Guangdong, where he was briefed on local government's efforts in poverty relief and rural reform.

Xi said the unbalanced development between urban and rural areas and among different regions was the biggest challenge of Guangdong's high-quality development.

"Strengthened, continued efforts and more targeted measures are needed to solve the urban and rural divide to turn weakness into potential and widen development space," he said.

After leaving the industrial park, Xi came to a public service station in Lianzhang village in Lianjiangkou town where he learned about the work of strengthening primary-level Party organizations, poverty alleviation and public service for villagers.

At a toy workshop, he chatted with workers and said the most direct and effective way to alleviate poverty was through industrial development. It is also a long-term plan to help create jobs for local communities. He said outstanding Party members with high quality, integrity and a spirit of fairness must be selected to lead fellow villagers out of poverty and to a comfortable life.

"No one should be left alone on the road toward poverty alleviation and a moderate prosperous society. The mission should be fulfilled through work of generation by generation," he said.

On Wednesday, 24 Oct, morning, in the city of Shenzhen, Xi visited an exhibition marking the 40th anniversary of reform and opening-up achievement in Guangdong. He said the "groundbreaking" changes in the past 40 years had drawn worldwide attention.

"I visit Shenzhen as it marks the 40-year anniversary of opening-up and reform in order to tell the world that China will not stop its opening-up and reform. China will certainly deliver a bigger miracle that draws worldwide attention," he said.

"We should stay true to our founding mission of reform and opening-up, draw on successful experiences in the past 40 years and raise quality and level of opening-up and reform.

"We should be people-oriented. People's happiness should be the criteria for evaluating the result of opening-up and reform. The fruits of opening-up and reform should benefit the general public."

He asked Guangdong to continue to carry forward its pioneering spirit and generate more experiences based on its own advantages, and hold the banner of opening-up and reform in a steadier and higher manner.

Xi then visited Qianhai and Shekou areas of Shenzhen in the Guangdong Pilot Free Trade Zone to inspect local development.

"Reform and opening-up has been proved by practice the right path which we must consistently, unswervingly and unremittingly follow," he said. Xi called for solid efforts in developing Qianhai, to provide more practical and innovative reform measures and explore more duplicable practices.

He urged Shenzhen and Hong Kong to deepen cooperation to play a bigger role in building the Belt and Road, advance the development of Guangdong-Hong Kong-Macao Greater Bay Area and participate in international cooperation at higher levels.

By noon, Xi arrived at a local community in Shenzhen, where he learned about public service, Party building at the grassroots and community administration. He said that more resources, services and management should be channeled to the community to provide residents with standardized and sophisticated services so that their issues, big or small, could be resolved.

On Wednesday afternoon, Xi went to the provincial capital Guangzhou, where he visited the historic Xiguan neighborhood and Jinan University. After hearing a work report on Guangzhou's urban planning and construction, he pointed out the importance of protecting historical culture and highlighting local features in urban planning.

At Jinan University, Xi viewed a gallery showing the university's history and achievements and talked with students from Hong Kong, Macao, and Taiwan and those who were overseas Chinese nationals. "China's connection with over 50 million overseas Chinese nationals is a unique advantage in its development," Xi said, noting that overseas Chinese nationals should also share some credit in China's reform and opening up. Xi expressed his hope that the university faculty could better run the college and create better conditions for overseas Chinese nationals to come to the motherland to study and carry forward Chinese culture.

During a visit to Guangzhou Mino Automotive Equipment Co. Ltd, Xi said private businesses had made great contributions to China's economic growth and had a very promising future.

"The CPC Central Committee always values the development of the non-public sector of the economy and is supportive of them, which has not changed and will not change," he said. "We will create better conditions for the development of private businesses and small and medium-sized enterprises."

On Thursday afternoon, Xi was briefed by officials of the CPC Guangdong Provincial Committee and the provincial government about their work, acknowledging the progress they had made.

"The development of Guangdong in the past four decades proved that reform and opening-up is the sure way to uphold and develop socialism with Chinese characteristics and decides China's fate," Xi said.

Instructing the province to deepen reform and opening-up, Xi said concrete efforts were needed to develop the Guangdong-Hong Kong-Macao Greater Bay Area, bring opening-up to a higher level and the Guangdong pilot free trade zone to a high standard.

Stressing high-quality development, Xi asked the province to expand real economy, enhance environmental protection, improve people's livelihoods, and encourage enterprises to play an active part in innovation.

Underlining balanced and coordinated development, he instructed the province to speed up rural vitalization, work for the coordinated development of different regions and promote rule of law.

Asking the province to strengthen Party leadership and Party building, Xi said they should firmly safeguard the authority and centralized, unified leadership of the CPC Central Committee, strictly enforce political discipline and rules, adopt the right approach in selecting and appointing officials, regulate officials' exchanges with business people, and form a new type of cordial and clean relationship between government and business.

BEIJING, 29 October 2018 (Xinhua) -- Xi Jinping, general secretary of the Communist Party of China (CPC) Central Committee, on Monday, 29 Oct, called for mobilizing the country's hundreds of millions of workers to make accomplishments in the new era, and break new ground in the cause of the workers' movement and trade unions' work.

Xi, also Chinese president and chairman of the Central Military Commission, made the remarks during a talk with the new leadership of the All-China Federation of Trade Unions (ACFTU).

The Workers' movement is an important part of the cause of the Party, while trade unions' work is a regular and fundamental job for the Party's governance, Xi said.

He urged upholding Party leadership over trade unions' work, mobilizing hundreds of millions of workers to make accomplishments in the new era, strengthening ideological and political guidance for employees, and advancing reforms and innovations in trade unions' work. He told the ACFTU leadership to be brave to shoulder responsibilities, be enterprising and active, and make solid efforts to break new ground in the cause of workers' movement and trade unions' work in the new era.

Xi, on behalf of the CPC Central Committee, congratulated the new leadership on the success of the 17th National Congress of the ACFTU, and greeted workers, model workers, and trade union workers of all ethnic groups.

Commenting on the work of the ACFTU and trade unions at all levels in the past five years, Xi said they made a lot of productive efforts in strengthening political guidance for workers, organizing employees' work, protecting workers' rights and interests, keeping the team of employees stable, deepening trade union reforms and innovations, and advancing Party building in the trade union system.

Trade unions should be loyal to the Party's cause and put the principle of upholding Party leadership and the Chinese socialist system into the practice of workers, Xi said. He stressed upholding the authority and centralized, unified leadership of the CPC Central Committee, and closely following political stance, direction, principle and path of the committee. Trade unions should improve their ability to apply the Marxist stance, viewpoint and method to analyze and solve problems, he said.

They should align the firm implementation of the Party's will with effective efforts to serve the workers, he said. Xi said the working class should be fully utilized as the main force to accomplish the targets proposed at the 19th CPC National Congress.

He encouraged the country's workers to devote themselves to their jobs, strive for excellence, and make unremitting efforts to create a happy life and a bright future.

Various competitions should be held with the theme of fostering new development philosophy, promoting high-quality development and building a modernized economy, he said. Faster work should be done to build a team of knowledgeable, skillful and innovative industrial workers, he said. He also demanded efforts to cultivate more model and highly-skilled workers.

It is the political responsibility of trade unions to guide employees and the people in following the Party, and consolidate the class foundation and public support for the Party's governance, Xi said. Although the times have changed, the work method of coming from the people and going to the people should not be changed, he said.

Trade unions should adapt to new situations and new tasks, he said. They should improve and strengthen ideological and political work for workers, and make more efforts to inspire the country's workers to embrace shared ideals, convictions, values and moral standards, Xi said. Rural workers should be included in trade unions to the largest extent to make them a new staunch and reliable force behind the working class, he said. Online work should be taken as an important platform for trade unions to link and serve the workers and to raise their penetration, guidance and influence, he said.

Trade unions should adhere to the employee-centered working approach; focus on the most pressing, most immediate issues that concern the employees the most; and fulfill the obligation of safeguarding workers' rights and interests and sincerely serving workers and the people, Xi said.

Work should also be done to help urban employees in difficulties out of trouble and offer timely assistance to employees who returned to poverty for different reasons, he said. As the reform of trade unions is an important component of deepening overall reform, trade unions should meet the new requirements on reforming people's organizations, and create a working system of extensive connection to serve the workers, Xi said.

More strength and resources should be put into the community level to unite all workers around the Party, he said.

Meanwhile, the country will reinforce the education, management and supervision of trade union cadres, and improve the mechanism of linking the Party with workers and the people, he said.

Party committees and governments at all levels must implement the Party's principle of wholeheartedly relying on the working class, and ensure the status of the working class as the master, Xi said.

The country should also improve and strengthen the Party's leadership on the work of trade unions, move to resolve major problems in the work of those unions, build a quality and professional team of trade union cadres, and support the creative work of trade unions in accordance with laws and regulations, he added.

BEIJING, 31 October 2018 (Xinhua) -- Xi Jinping, general secretary of the Communist Party of China (CPC) Central Committee, has stressed boosting the development of the country's new generation of artificial intelligence (AI).

Presiding over a group study session of the Political Bureau of the CPC Central Committee on Wednesday, 31 Oct, Xi spoke of the need to strengthen leadership, make good plans, clearly define tasks, and consolidate the foundation to promote deep integration of AI with economic and social development.

Xi said accelerating the development of new-generation AI is a strategic issue, key for China to seize the opportunities in the new round of technological revolution and industrial transformation.

Accelerating the development of new-generation AI is a key strategic resource for China, to boost leapfrogging development in science and technology, industrial upgrading, and overall productivity increase, he said. Xi spoke of the need to prioritize enhancing ability for original innovations, and focus on key core technologies. He said China supports scientists venturing into unknown AI frontiers to achieve breakthroughs. He said key core AI technologies should be "securely kept in our own hands."

Xi said China has a pressing need for major innovations in fields such as new-generation AI, as the country is in a pivotal stage for transforming its growth model, improving economic structure, and creating new drivers of growth.

A deeper integration of AI and industrial development can provide new power for high quality growth, he said. Xi highlighted the need for fostering leading AI enterprises and sectors.

He called for integration of AI with primary, secondary, and tertiary industries, to create new growth drivers in medium-high end consumption, innovation-driven development, the green and low-carbon economy, the sharing economy, modern supply chains, and human capital services. Xi said it was necessary to combine AI with improving living standards. He said AI should be used in areas such as education, health, sports, housing, transport, disabled and old-age care, and housekeeping. Xi said risk analysis in AI development should be strengthened, and precautions stepped up, to secure the people's interests and national security. It must be made sure that AI is safe, reliable and controllable, he said.

Xi also stressed the need to establish and improve laws, regulations, institutions, and ethics to ensure healthy development of AI.

He urged officials at all levels to work to learn cutting-edge science and technology, strengthen coordination, and increase policy support.

  Hong Kong. (Population 7.3 M, rank 104, growth 0.8%. Partly Free: 61 of 100).

  Macau (Population 622 K, rank 167, growth 1.7 %.)

Taiwan: (Population 23.6 M, rank 56, growth 0.3%. Free, 91 of 100).

Japan (Population 127.5 M, rank 11, decrease 0.2%. Free, 96 of 100). 26 October 2018. Reports: Calling it an "historic turning point," China and Japan have pledged to forge closer ties, signing a broad range of agreements including a $30 B currency swap pact, amid rising trade tensions with Washington. Asia's two biggest economies also agreed to boost cooperation in the securities markets like the listing of ETFs and signed a deal towards establishing a yuan clearing bank, as the renminbi slipped to its lowest against the dollar in a decade.

31 October 2018. Reports: The Bank of Japan opted to hold rates at -0.1% at its October meeting, while trimming inflation forecasts and saying it will purchase 10-year Japanese government bonds to maintain the yield at "around zero percent." This will see the BOJ fall even further behind global peers in normalizing policy, amid its long battle to stoke inflation, which it now expects to remain below its 2% target until at least early 2021.

Japan, Kyoto (678): the hall gate of the founder of the Shinshu Honbyo Temple (1321, until 1987 Higashi Hongan-Ji, total area 99,000 m^2), viewed from a round water garden in the middle of Karasuma Dori, north of Shichijo Dori, south of Hanayacho Dori.

Afghanistan: (Population 35.5 M, rank 40, growth 2.5%. Not free: 24 of 100).

South Korea: (Population 50.9 M, rank 27, growth 0.4%. Free, 82 of 100). Reports: The two Koreas have taken another step toward peace, removing landmines along the heavily fortified border. Guard posts are also coming down in the so-called Joint Security Area, with the troops remaining there to be left unarmed. Project details were agreed during last month's summit in Pyongyang, where Kim Jong-un met South Korean President Moon Jae-in.

North Korea: (Population 25.4 M, rank 52, growth 0.5%. Not free: 3 of 100).

Vietnam (Population 95.5 M, rank 15, growth 1%. Not free, 20 of 100). 23 October 2018. Vladimir Putin congratulated Nguyen Phu Trong on his election as President of the Socialist Republic of Vietnam.

Laos (Population. 6.8 M, rank 106, growth 1.5%. Not free: 12 of 100).

Cambodia (Population 16 M, rank 71, growth 1.5%. Not Free 31 of 100).

Mongolia (Population 3 M, rank 137, growth 1.6%. Free 85 of 100)

Nepal: (Population 29.3 M, rank 48, growth 1.1%. Partly free 52 of 100).

Russia, Switzerland, Eastern Europe

Russia: (Population 143.9 M, rank 9, growth 0%. Not free: 20 of 100). Reports: In the 1990s, Russia experimented with using an orbital mirror to reflect sunlight on some of its Sun-deprived northern cities, according to the New York Times. The project was abandoned in 1999, after the mirror failed to unfold, and was incinerated in the atmosphere.

23 October 2018. Vladimir Putin received in the Kremlin Assistant to the President of the United States of America for National Security Affairs, John Bolton.

Taking part in the meeting from the Russian side were Presidential Aide Yury Ushakov, Foreign Minister Sergei Lavrov and Security Council Secretary Nikolai Patrushev.

Earlier today, Russian Defense Minister Sergei Shoigu met with John Bolton. On October 22, Nikolai Patrushev and Sergei Lavrov also had talks with the Assistant to the US President.

Beginning of conversation with Assistant to the US President for National Security Affairs, John Bolton.

President of Russia, Vladimir Putin: Mr. Bolton, colleagues,

We are pleased to see you in Moscow. At the beginning of our conversation I would like to recall our meeting with the President of the United States in Helsinki. In my view, it was a useful, and at times fairly tough, meeting and conversation which ultimately turned out to be fruitful, in my opinion.

This is why, to be honest, we are sometimes perplexed to see the United States take absolutely unprovoked steps towards Russia that we cannot call friendly. We actually do not even respond to your steps, yet this approach continues.

Despite your efforts trade between our countries – however strange it might seem – continues to grow, 16% last year; this year it has already grown by 8%. This is small in absolute numbers, very small, of course, however, this is the trend. With a positive balance for the United States, by the way. Mutual investments are also growing with Russian investments in the US economy at twice the US investments in the Russian economy.

It will, of course, be very useful to exchange views on the issues of strategic stability, disarmament issues, and regional conflicts.

We know – and talk a lot – about the unilateral exit of the United States from the Anti-Ballistic Missile Treaty. We recently heard about the United States' intention to exit the Intermediate-Range Nuclear Forces Treaty. We know about the Administration's doubts about prolonging New START, and hear about the intention to deploy some elements of the anti-missile defense system in space.

As I recall, there is a bald eagle pictured on the US coat of arms: it holds 13 arrows in one talon, and an olive branch in the other, as a symbol of peaceful policy: a branch with 13 olives. My question: has your eagle already eaten all the olives leaving only the arrows?

In general, I would like very much to talk with you not only as the Assistant to the US President, but also as a specialist on disarmament and arms control.

And, of course, it would be useful to continue a direct dialogue with the US President, first of all, on the sidelines of the international events that will take place soon, such as the one in Paris. Of course, if the US is interested in such contacts.

Assistant to the President of the United States of America for National Security Affairs, John Bolton: Well, thank you very much, Mr. President. It is a pleasure to see you again. I appreciate you taking the time to get together, and will be pleased to go over all the items on the agenda. And to begin, as you indicated, I think President Trump will look forward to seeing you in Paris, on the sidelines of the celebration of the 100th anniversary of the Armistice. Because, despite our differences, which exist because of our different national interests, it is still important to work in areas where there is a possibility of mutual cooperation. And I had discussions with all of your senior national security advisors in the past two days, and again, I am grateful for the opportunity to speak with you, on behalf of President Trump. And hopefully, I'll have some answers for you, but I didn't bring any olives.

Vladimir Putin: My thoughts exactly. (Laughter.)

John Bolton: The olive branch is held in the right talon of the eagle, demonstrating its priority.

Vladimir Putin: If I remember correctly, there is also an inscription: In Varietate Concordia, United in Diversity. This is why, despite different approaches, we can and should look for points of contact.

John Bolton: That's very much our intention, though our motto is "E pluribus unum," "Out of many, one," so maybe it is something to look forward to there.

25 October 2018. Reports: Vladimir Putin has warned of a new arms race if America pulls out of the three-decade-old Intermediate-Range Nuclear Forces Treaty, saying Russia would target European countries, if they host U.S. nuclear missiles. NATO Secretary-General. Jens Stoltenberg. said he didn't believe the Russian threat would lead to new U.S. missile deployments to Europe.

Switzerland: (Population 8.4 M, rank 99, growth 0.9%. Free: 96 of 100). Reports: Numbered bank accounts have officially ended in Switzerland, the world's biggest center for managing offshore wealth. Swiss authorities have begun automatically sharing client data with tax agencies in dozens of other countries - under global standards that aim to crack down on tax cheats - and will expand next year to about 80 states.

Austria: (Population 8.7 M, rank 98, growth 0.3%. Free: 95 of 100). 4 October 2018. President of Russia Vladimir Putin and Federal Chancellor of Austria Sebastian Kurz visited the State Hermitage Museum. In St Petersburg, Vladimir Putin had talks with Federal Chancellor of the Republic of Austria Sebastian Kurz, who is in Russia on a working visit.
The President and the Chancellor discussed the status and development prospects of Russia-Austria relations, topical international and regional problems, and Austria's Presidency of the Council of the European Union in the second half of 2018.

History: On November 12, Austria will celebrate 100 years since the proclamation of the Republic of Austria.

26 October 2018. Vladimir Putin congratulated Federal President of the Republic of Austria, Alexander Van der Bellen, and Federal Chancellor of the Republic of Austria, Sebastian Kurz, on the country's national holiday – the anniversary of adopting the Constitutional Law on the Neutrality of Austria.
The message reads, in part: "I am pleased to note the constructive nature of Russian-Austrian relations. I am confident that through joint efforts we will further develop bilateral dialogue and fruitful

cooperation in various fields, for the benefit of the peoples of our countries, and in the interests of strengthening European security and stability."

Poland: (Population 38.1 M, rank 37, decrease 0.1%. Free: 89 of 100).

Croatia: (Population 4.1 M, rank 129, decrease 0.6%. Free: 87 of 100).

Finland: (Population 5.5 M, rank 116, growth 0.4%. Free: 100 of 100).

Romania (Population: 19.6 M, rank 59, decrease 0.5%. Free: 84 of 100)

Moldova: (Population: 4 M, rank 132, decrease 0.2%. Partly Free: 62 of 100). 31 October 2018. In Moscow, Vladimir Putin met with President of the Republic of Moldova, Igor Dodon, who arrived in Russia on an official visit, to discuss Russia-Moldova interaction in trade, the economy and culture, as well as important regional issues.

Belarus: (Population: 9.4 M, rank 93, decrease 0.1%. Not Free: 20 of 100).

Bulgaria: (Population: 7 M, rank 105, decrease 0.7%. Free: 80 of 100).

Slovenia: (Population: 2 M, rank 148, growth 0.1%. Free: 92 of 100).

Hungary: (Population: 9.7 M, rank 91, decrease 0.3%. Free: 76 of 100)

Ukraine: (Population: 44.2 M, rank 32, decrease 0.5%. Partly free: 61 of 100).

Latvia: (Population: 1.9 M, rank 150, decrease 1.1%. Free: 87 of 100).

Lithuania: (Population: 2.8 M, rank 141, decrease 0.6%. Free: 91 of 100).

Estonia: (Population: 1.3 M, rank 155, decrease 0.2%. Free: 94 of 100).

Serbia: (including Kosovo: Population: 8.7 M, rank 97, decrease 0.3%. Free: 76 of 100).

Kosovo ((Disputed: recognized by 110 countries, and not recognized by Serbia, Russia, and others) Population: 1.8 M, Partly free: 52 of 100).

Turkey: (Population 80.7 M, rank 19, growth 1.2%. Partly free: 38 of 100). 27 October 2018. Vladimir Putin met with President of Turkey, Recep Tayyip Erdogan, in Istanbul.
The conversation was held at Vahdettin Pavilion, which will later host a meeting of the leaders of Russia, Turkey, Germany and France.
27 October 2018. President of Russia Vladimir Putin, President of Turkey Recep Tayyip Erdogan, Federal Chancellor of Germany Angela Merkel and President of France Emmanuel Macron had a meeting in Istanbul. The leaders shared opinions on Syria, including ways to promote the political settlement process.
Following the talks Vladimir Putin, Recep Tayyip Erdogan, Angela Merkel and Emmanuel Macron adopted a Joint Statement.
Following the talks, Vladimir Putin, Recep Tayyip Erdogan, Angela Merkel and Emmanuel Macron held a joint news conference.
29 October 2018. The President of Russia sent his greetings to President of Turkey, Recep Tayyip Erdogan, on the 95th anniversary of the establishment of the Republic of Turkey.

Greece: (Population 11.1 M, rank 82, decrease 0.2%. Free: 84 of 100).

Republic of North Macedonia: (Population 2 M, rank 147, growth 0.1%. Partly Free: 57 of 100).

Albania: (Population 2.9 M, rank 139, growth 0.1%. Partly free: 68 of 100).

Cyprus: (Population 1.1 M, rank 159, growth 0.8%. Free: 94 of 100).

Kazakhstan (Population 18.2 M, rank 64, growth 1.2%. Not free: 22 of 100. 20 October 2018. During his informal meeting with President of Kazakhstan, Nursultan Nazarbayev, and President of Uzbekistan, Shavkat Mirziyoyev, in the city of Saryagash in Kazakhstan's Turkestan Region, Vladimir Putin discussed matters of trilateral economic and humanitarian cooperation, and other urgent issues.

Armenia: (Population 2.9 M, rank 138, growth 0.2%. Partly free: 45 of 100).

Azerbaijan: (Population 9.8 M, rank 90, growth 1.1%. Not free 14 of 100).

Uzbekistan: (Population 31.9 M, rank 44, growth 1.5%. Not free: 3 of 100). 19 October 2018. Vladimir Putin had talks with President of Uzbekistan, Shavkat Mirziyoyev, in Tashkent.

Kyrgyzstan (Population 6 M, rank 112, growth 1.5%. Partly free, 37 of 100).

Tajikistan: (Population 8.9 M, rank 96, growth 2.1%. Not free, 11 of 100).

Turkmenistan: (Population 5.7 M, rank 113, growth 1.7%. Not free, 4 of 100).

Japan Tokyo (1150): In Shinjuku, Shinjuku Center Bldg (223 m, 54 fl, 1979, left), Mode Gakuen Cocoon Tower (204 m, 50 fl, 2008, center), Keio Plaza Hotel North Tower (180 m, 47 fl, 1971, right).

United Kingdom, Canada, South America

United Kingdom: (Population: 66.1 M, rank 21, growth 0.6%. Free: 95 of 100).

Ireland: (Population: 4.7 M, rank 123, growth 0.8%. Free: 96 of 100) Reports: The Irish Data Protection Commissioner has opened a formal investigation into the recent cybercriminals' attack at Facebook that affected nearly 50 M accounts. According to new GDPR legislation, firms can be hit with fines if they are found to have not done enough to prevent a data breach. The maximum penalty Facebook could face is 4% of annual global turnover, an amount which could total around $1.63B.

Canada: (Population: 36.6 M, rank 38, growth 0.9%. Free: 99 of 100).

Canada, Niagara Falls: the American Falls (21-30 m drop, 290 m wide), the Bridal Veil Falls (right, 21m), after Luna Island.

Mexico: (Population: 129.1 M, rank 10, growth 1.3%. Partly Free: 65 of 100).

Chile: (Population: 18 M, rank 65, growth 0.8%. Free 94 of 100).

Colombia: (Population: 49 M, rank 29, growth 0.8%. Partly free 64 of 100).

Argentina: (Population: 44.2 M, rank 31, growth, 1%. Free: 82 of 100).

Brazil (Population: 209.2 M, rank 6, growth 0.8%. Free, 79 of 100). 29 October 2018. Reports: Jair Bolsonaro has comfortably won Brazil's presidential election with 55% of the vote, in a victory that reflected widespread anger at the political class after years of corruption, and an ailing economy.

29 October 2018. Vladimir Putin sent Jair Bolsonaro a message congratulating him on winning the presidential elections in the Federative Republic of Brazil.

Peru: (Population: 32.1 M, rank 5, growth 1.2%. Free: 72 of 100)

Cuba: (Population: 11.4 M, rank 42, growth 0.1%. Not free, 15 of 100).

Bolivia: (Population: 11 M, rank 83, growth 1.5%. Partly free 68 of 100).

Paraguay: (Population: 6.8 M, rank 107, growth 1.3%. Partly free 64 of 100).

Panama: (Population: 4.1 M, rank 131, growth 1.6%. Free: 83 of 100).

Venezuela: (Population: 32 M, rank 43, growth 1.3%. Not free: 30 of 100).

Guyana: (Population 777K, (rank 165, grows 0.6%). Free: 74 of 100).

Trinidad and Tobago: (Population 1.3 M, (rank 153, grows 0.3%). Free: 81 of 100).

Nicaragua: (Population 6.2 M, (rank 110, grows 1.1%). Partly Free: 47 of 100).

Japan: Mount Fuji (3,776 m, 1707 last eruption), from 17 km north in Kawaguchiko city (Lake Kawaguchi, 6 km^2, 830 m elevation).

France, Germany, and neighbors

France: (Population 64.9 M, rank 22, growth 0.4%. Free: 90 of 100). 27 October 2018. Vladimir Putin had a telephone conversation with President of the French Republic, Emmanuel Macron, at the French side's initiative.

Belgium (Population 11.4 M, rank 80, growth 0.6%. Free: 95 of 100)

European Commission, European Union, EU: 28 EU countries: Austria, Belgium, Bulgaria, Croatia, Republic of Cyprus, Czech Republic, Denmark, Estonia, Finland, France, Germany, Greece, Hungary, Ireland, Italy, Latvia, Lithuania, Luxembourg, Malta, Netherlands, Poland, Portugal, Romania, Slovakia, Slovenia, Spain, Sweden and the UK.

Germany: (Population 82.1 M, rank 16, growth 0.2%. Free: 95 of 100). 4 October 2018. Vladimir Putin sent greetings to Federal President of the Federal Republic of Germany, Frank-Walter Steinmeier, and Federal Chancellor Angela Merkel on the Day of German Unity.

27 October 2018. President of Russia Vladimir Putin and Chancellor of the Federal Republic of Germany, Angela Merkel, had a bilateral meeting in Istanbul.

Norway (Population 5.3 M, rank 118, growth 1%. Free: 100 of 100).

Sweden (Population 9.9 M, rank 89, growth 0.7%. Free: 100 of 100).

The Netherlands (Population 17 M, rank 67, growth 0.3%. Free: 99 of 100).

Czech Republic (Population 10.6 M, rank 87, growth 0.1%. Free: 94 of 100). 29 October 2018. Vladimir Putin sent greetings to the President of the Czech Republic, Milos Zeman, on Independent Czechoslovak State Day.

Denmark (Population 5.7 M, rank 114, growth 0.4%. Free: 97 of 100).

Luxembourg (Population 583 K, rank 169, growth 1.3%. Free: 98 of 100).

Spain: (Population 46.3 M, rank 30, growth 0%. Free: 94 of 100).

Portugal: (Population 10.3 M, rank 88, decrease 0.4%. Free: 97 of 100).

India, Pakistan, Australia, and neighbors

India (Population: 1.3 B, rank 2nd, growth 1.1%. Free: 77 of 100). 4 October 2018. Vladimir Putin arrived in India on an official visit. Vladimir Putin met with Prime Minister of the Republic of India, Narendra Modi, in New Delhi.
Vladimir Putin met with President of India, Ram Nath Kovind.
19 October 2018. Vladimir Putin conveyed his condolences to President of India Ram Nath Kovind, and Prime Minister of India Narendra Modi, on the tragic aftermath of the railway accident in Punjab.

Indonesia: (Population: 263.9 M, rank 4, growth 1.1%. Partly free: 65 of 100). 29 October 2018. Vladimir Putin sent a message of condolences to President of Indonesia, Joko Widodo, on the death of passengers and crew in a plane crash off Java.

Australia: (Population: 24.4 M, rank 53, growth 1.3%. Free: 98 of 100).

New Zealand: (Population 4.7 M, rank 125, growth 1%. Free: 98 of 100).

Pakistan: (Population 212 M, rank 5, growth 2%. Partly free: 43 of 100

Philippines: (Population 104.9 M, rank 13, growth 1.5%. Partly free 63 of 100).

Singapore: (Population 5.7 M, rank 115, growth 1.5%. Partly free 51 of 100).

Thailand: (Population 69 M, rank 20, growth 0.3%. Not free 32 of 100).

Myanmar (Burma, Population 53.3 M, rank 26, growth 0.9%. Not free 32 of 100

Bangladesh (Population 164.6 M, rank 8, growth 1.1%. Partly free 47 of 100).

Sri Lanka (Population 20.8 M, rank 58, growth 0.4%. Partly free 56 of 100). 29 October 2018. Reports: A political crisis in Sri Lanka took a deadly turn yesterday, 28 Oct. One person was killed when a sacked cabinet minister tried to re-enter his office, days after the president removed the prime minister, and installed a powerful Chinese ally in his place.

Malaysia (Population 31.6 M, rank 45, growth 1.34%. Partly free 44 of 100).

Brunei: (Population 428,000, rank 176, growth 1.3%. Not free 29 of 100).

Vanuatu: (Population 276,000, rank 185, growth 2.2%. Free 80 of 100)

Italy, Middle East, Africa

Italy: (Population 59.3 M, rank 23, decrease 0.1%. Free: 89 of 100). 15 October 2018. Reports: Italy's government signed off on an expansionary deficit 2019 budget late Monday, 15 October - with planned measures that would boost welfare spending, lower the retirement age, and cut taxes - in defiance of EU rules that require a shrinking deficit. The draft budget law has rattled financial markets in the past month, with investors demanding significantly higher interest rates to buy Italian bonds.

23 October 2018. Reports: "There isn't any B plan," Italian Prime Minister Giuseppe Conte told Bloomberg as the European Commission formally rejected Italy's draft budget. "I said that the deficit at 2.4% of GDP is the cap. I can say this will be our cap." While actual sanctions are improbable and wouldn't be levied for months, European officials have also been wary of handing more ammunition to Italy's Eurosceptic government.

24 October 2018. Vladimir Putin met with Prime Minister of the Italian Republic, Giuseppe Conte, who is in Russia on an official visit. The parties exchanged opinions on expanding bilateral cooperation in energy, investment, culture, the humanitarian sphere, and other areas. Vladimir Putin and Giuseppe Conte also discussed a range of international and regional matters, including developments in Syria and Libya, as well as the two countries' cooperation in the Organization for Security and Cooperation in Europe (OSCE) in light of Italy's 2018 OSCE chairmanship.

Vatican: (Population 792, rank 233 (last), decrease 1.1%).

San Marino: (Population 33,400, rank 218, growth 0.6%. Free 97 of 100)

Italy, Rome (753 BC): Sapienza – Università di Roma, founded in 1303. Signs on the campus: Matematica, Fisica, Filosofia, Ortopedia to the right, Aula Magna, Mineralogia to the left.

Jordan (Population 9.7 M, rank 92, growth 2.6%. Partly free, 37 of 100). 26 October 2018. Vladimir Putin sent his condolences to King Abdullah II of the Hashemite Kingdom of Jordan over a tour bus swept away in a Dead Sea flash flood.

Lebanon: (Population: 6 M, rank 111, growth 1.3%. Partly free: 44 of 100).

United Arab Emirates (UAE) (Population: 9.4 M, rank 94, growth 1.4%. Not free, 20 of 100).

Saudi Arabia (Population 32.9 M, rank 41, growth 2.1%. Not free: 10 of 100). Reports: Russia and Saudi Arabia struck a private deal in September to raise oil output.

25 October 2018. Vladimir Putin had a telephone conversation with King of Saudi Arabia, Salman bin Abdulaziz Al Saud, at the Saudi side's initiative.

The issues of the further development of multifaceted bilateral cooperation, including in the energy sector, were thoroughly discussed. King Salman confirmed his invitation to Vladimir Putin to visit Saudi Arabia. It was agreed to work out the terms of such a visit through diplomatic channels.

The leaders exchanged views on the Syrian issue, and the state of affairs in the Middle East in general. The situation around the 'Jamal Khashoggi case' was also addressed.

Yemen (Population 28.2 M, rank 50, growth 2.4%. Not free: 14 of 100).

Iraq (Population 38.2 M, rank 36, growth 2.9%. Not free: 27 of 100). 25 October 2018. Reports. Iraq's new prime minister has been sworn into office after lawmakers approved a majority of his cabinet, giving the country a government five months after elections. The session highlighted the challenges that Adel Abdul-Mahdi faces in fixing a dysfunctional political system, while revamping Iraq's struggling oil-dependent economy, and rebuilding infrastructure destroyed in the war against ISIS.

Iran: (Population 81.1 M, rank 18, growth 1.1%. Not free: 17 of 100.

Israel: (Population 8.3 M, rank 100, growth 1.6%. Free: 80 of 100).

Palestine: (Population 4.9 M (rank 121, grows 2.7%). Not free: 28 of 100).

Egypt (Population 97.5 M (rank 14, grows 1.9%). Not free, 26 of 100). 16 October 2018. Vladimir Putin and Abdel Fattah el-Sisi had an informal meeting in Sochi, Russia.

17 October 2018. In Sochi, Russia, Vladimir Putin held talks with President of the Arab Republic of Egypt, Abdel Fattah el-Sisi, who is in Russia on an official visit. Following the consultations, Vladimir Putin and Abdel Fattah el-Sisi signed the Agreement on Comprehensive Partnership and Strategic Cooperation between the Russian Federation and the Arab Republic of Egypt.

League of Arab States (LAS) (22 countries: Algeria, Bahrein, Comoros, Djibouti, Egypt, Iraq, Jordan, Kuwait, Lebanon, Libya, Mauritania, Morocco, Oman, Palestine, Qatar, Saudi Arabia, Somalia, Sudan, Syria, Tunisia, United Arab Emirates and Yemen).

Qatar: (Population 2.6 M (rank 142, grows 2.7%). Not free: 26 of 100).

Kuwait: (Population 4.1 M (rank 130, grows 2.1%). Partly free: 36 of 100).

Oman: (Population 4.6 M (rank 127, grows 4.8%). Not free: 25 of 100)

Bahrain: (Population 1.5 M (rank 152, grows 4.7%). Not free: 12 of 100).

Syria: (Population 18.2 M (rank 63, decrease 0.9%). Not free: 0 of 100).

Kenya: (Population 49.7 M (rank 28, growth 2.6%. Partly free, 51 of 100).

Libya: (Population 6.3 M, rank 109, growth 1.3%. Not free: 13 of 100).

Tunisia: (Population 11.5 M, rank 78, growth 1.1%. Free: 78 of 100).

Morocco: (Population 35.7 M, rank 39, growth 1.3%. Partly free: 41 of 100).

South Africa: (Population 56.7 M, rank 25, growth 1.3%. Free, 78 of 100). 26 October 2018. Reports: South African President Cyril Ramaphosa is seeking $100 B of new investments over the next five years, and has already secured pledges for around $35 B, mainly from China, Saudi Arabia and the UAE. When he took over in February, Ramaphosa staked his reputation on economic revival and his strong ties to the business community. But since then, the economy has sunk into recession, and faced a series of downbeat data.

Zimbabwe: (Population 16.5 M, rank 70, growth 2.4%. Partly Free, 32 of 100).

Sudan (Population 40.5 M, rank 35, growth 2.4%. Not Free: 6 of 100).

South Sudan (Population 12.5 M, rank 76, growth 2.8%. Not Free: 4 of 100)

Guinea: (Population 12.7 M, rank 75, growth 2.6%. Partly Free, 41 of 100).

Djibouti (Population 957,000, rank 160, growth 1.6%. Not Free: 26 of 100).

Somalia: (Population 14.7 M, rank 74, growth 3%. Not free: 5 of 100).

Niger (Population 21.4 M, rank 57, growth 3.9%. Partly free: 49 of 100).

Nigeria (Population 190.8 M, rank 7, growth 2.6%. Partly free: 50 of 100).

Cameroon (Population 24 M, rank 55, growth 2.6%. Not free: 24 of 100).

Sierra Leone: (Population 7.5 M (rank 103, grows 2.2%). Partly free: 66 of 100)

Chad: (Population 15 M (rank 73, grows 3.1%). Not free: 18 of 100).

The Gambia: (Population 2.1 M (rank 146, grows 3%). Not free: 20 of 100).

Malawi: (Population 18.6 M (rank 61, grows 2.9%). Partly free: 63 of 100).

Rwanda: (Population 12.2 M (rank 77, grows 2.4%). Not free: 24 of 100).

Burkina Faso: (Population 19.1 M (rank 60, grows 2.9%). Partly free: 63 of 100).

Central African Republic: (Population 4.6 M (rank 126, grows 1.4%). Not free: 10 of 100).

Senegal: (Population 15.8 M (rank 72, grows 2.8%). Free: 78 of 100).

Gabon: (Population 2 M (rank 149, grows 2.3%). Partly Free: 32 of 100).

Madagascar: (Population 25.5 M (rank 51, grows 2.7%). Partly Free: 56 of 100).

Democratic Republic of the Congo: (Population 81.3 M (rank 17, grows 3.3%). Not Free: 19 of 100).

Angola: (Population 29.7 M (rank 46, grows 3.4%). Not Free: 24 of 100).

Zambia: (Population 17 M (rank 66, grows 3%). Partly Free: 56 of 100).

United Republic of Tanzania: (Population 57 M (rank 24, grows 3.1%). Partly Free: 58 of 100).

Canada, Niagara Falls: Niagara River on the west end of the Horseshoe Falls (in Canada, 53 m drop, 790 m wide).

Medical

A new robot could revive an abandoned prostatectomy procedure, said a Cleveland Clinic surgeon, mentioning the future potential of a new single-port robotic system.

Harvard researchers did an experiment. They gave one group of people an electronic tablet to read before bed, and the other group received a book. After 5 days of monitoring the two groups their findings confirmed their suspicions: the participants who read the tablet before bedtime reported: more difficulty falling asleep, more restless sleep, and feeling more tired the next day.
Not only that — the blood tests of the tablet group showed *less melatonin* in their body than the book readers.
The National Sleep Foundation recommends shutting off your smartphone about 1-2 hours before bedtime.
That way, the body can begin countering the effects of blue light exposure throughout the day and prepare for rest - when you avoid this screen-time, your body will experience a significant boost in melatonin — up to 58%.

Americans consume too few fruits and vegetables for optimal health: In fact, more than 75% do not meet the USDA's recommended intake (2.5 cups of vegetables and 2 cups of fruit a day, for a 2,000-calorie daily diet).

For yet another year, strawberries topped the list of produce with the highest pesticide residues, followed by spinach, nectarines, apples, grapes, peaches, cherries, pears, tomatoes, celery, potatoes, and sweet bell peppers.
The produce with the lowest pesticide residues are avocados, sweet corn, pineapples, cabbage, onions, sweet peas (frozen), papayas, asparagus, mangoes, eggplant, honeydew melon, kiwi, cantaloupe, cauliflower, and broccoli.

Despite more than a century of scientific endeavor, influenza remains one of the deadliest infectious diseases worldwide. Across Europe, many biotechs are working on new solutions that could dramatically improve the protection rates offered by current vaccines. Some may even lead to the end objective of the influenza research – a universal flu vaccine.

A mathematical algorithm proves better than humans at controlling blood sugar in type 1 diabetes.

More than 90% of the medicine being practiced today did not exist in 1950. Two centuries ago medicine was still an art, not a science at all. As recently as the 1920s, long after the birth of modern medicine, there was usually little the medical profession could do, once disease set in, other than alleviate some of the symptoms, and let nature take its course. It was the patient's immune system that cured him, when it worked well.

Bose Corp. has developed a hearing aid that FDA said is the first device that enables users to fit, program, and control without the assistance from a health care provider.

In pharmaceutical companies, sophisticated automation enhances precision, flexibility, and product safety.

A single dose of Janssen 's Stelara induces clinical remission of ulcerative colitis.

Q BioMed begins preparations to test a drug targeting a patient subset on the autism spectrum.

Researcher develops 3-in-1 vaccine against traveler's diarrhea.

FDA oncologic drugs advisory committee recommends approval of proposed Rituximab biosimilar.

Researchers have developed techniques to detect Lyme disease bacteria weeks sooner than current tests, allowing patients to start treatment earlier. – Rutgers University-New Brunswick

Massachusetts General Hospital in Boston has 1.5 million annual outpatient visits.

BOSTON (October 15, 2018) – Harnessing the power of digital health technology --- smart phone apps, telemedicine and mobile health (m-health) --- can provide powerful tools to help people with diabetes self-management, and ultimately improving A1c level. – Joslin Diabetes Center, Cell Metabolism

Italy, Rome (753 BC): Amphitheatrum Flavium (70 - 80, nickname Colosseum), built by Flavius Vespasianus (9 - 79, emperor 69 - 79) and his son Titus Flavius (39 - 81, emperor 79 - 81).

The first generic version of the EpiPen has been approved by the U.S. Food and Drug Administration, paving the way for more affordable versions of the lifesaving allergy emergency medication.

Research shows people's diet and weight, and other lifestyle habits, can prevent up to 80% of heart attacks and strokes.

Researchers engineer a dual vaccine against anthrax and plague.

ISPOR—the professional society for health economics and outcomes research (HEOR), has published a new Good Practices for Outcomes Research Report that illustrates how constrained optimization methods can be used to assess the value of health technology. Value in Health, Sep-2018

FDA approved Pfizer's Talzenna for some patients with BRCA-Mutated breast cancer.

AstraZeneca and Merck obtain orphan drug designation for Lynparza for pancreatic cancer.

A Loyola University Chicago Stritch School of Medicine study reveals how, on a cellular level, diabetes can cause heart failure. The findings could lead to medications to treat and perhaps prevent heart failure in diabetes patients.
– Loyola University Health System, JCI Insight

Data on the molecular makeup and drug sensitivity of hundreds of patient samples could accelerate progress against the aggressive blood cancer acute myeloid leukemia.
– Howard Hughes Medical Institute (HHMI), Nature, Oct-2018

General information about some minerals – always ask your doctor first:
Calcium - Foods that have it: Milk, fortified nondairy alternatives like soy milk, yogurt, hard cheeses, fortified cereals, kale
How much: Adults ages 19-50: 1,000 milligrams per day
Women age 51 and older: 1,200 milligrams per day
Men age 51 - 70: 1,000 milligrams per day
Men 71 and older: 1,200 milligrams per day
What it does: Needed for bone growth and strength, blood clotting, muscle contraction, and more
No more than this a day: 2,500 milligrams per day for adults age 50 and younger, 2,000 mg per day for those 51 and older
Choline - Foods that have it: Milk, liver, eggs, peanuts
How much: Men: 550 milligrams per day
Women: 425 milligrams per day

Pregnant women: 450 milligrams per day
Breastfeeding women: 550 milligrams per day
What it does: Helps make cells
No more than this much: 3,500 milligrams per day

Gauss, a Los Altos, CA-based company has raised $20 M to use AI to accurately measure blood loss.

Researcher has developed a method to genetically modify a patient's T-cells to specifically recognize and kill kidney cancer cells.

Shire receives unanimous FDA Advisory Committee approval recommendation for Prucalopride.

When it comes to preventing blood clots after a knee replacement, aspirin may be just as effective as newer, more expensive drugs, such as rivaroxaban (Xarelto), according to a study by University of Michigan orthopedic surgeons.
– Michigan Medicine - University of Michigan, JAMA Surgery

An additive manufactured cardiac patch may offer healing to patients with acute myocardial infarction, as well as pave the way for an entire human heart replacement.

Experimental drug Dapirolizumab Pegol fails in mid-stage lupus trial.

Researchers will present preliminary findings at the 60th Annual Meeting of the American Society for Radiation Oncology in San Antonio on Tuesday, Oct. 23, from a study which evaluated a blood test for HPV-linked oropharyngeal squamous cell carcinoma. The HPV blood test shows promise for tracking head and neck cancer after treatment.
– University of North Carolina Health Care System
American Society for Radiation Oncology 60th Annual Meeting

A pioneer in the study of neural cells revealed today (Oct. 23, 2018) how a single mutation, affecting the most common protein in a supporting brain cell, produces devastating, fibrous globs. These, in turn, disturb the location of cellular processing. – University of Wisconsin-Madison, Cell Reports October 23, 2018

A recent Rutgers study finds that parents educated beyond high school have healthier families, as they invest more in family health care, which reduces the likelihood of adverse medical conditions. Therefore, children health outcomes have more to do with parents' level of education than income.
– Rutgers University-New Brunswick

Nurses with bachelor's degrees report being very prepared in more quality and safety measures than do their peers with associate degrees, finds a new study by researchers at NYU Rory Meyers College of Nursing. – New York University
Joint Commission Journal on Quality and Patient Safety

There are over 7 billions of people alive right now. And each person has unique DNA, which carries hidden information about their health.

Pfizer creates Cerevel Therapeutics to focus on treating central nervous system disorders.

Alternate therapies for pain; the use of artificial intelligence in healthcare; and an expanded window to treat stroke patients are some of the innovations that will enhance healing and change healthcare in the coming year, according to a distinguished panel of doctors and researchers.

The Most Probable Number method can be useful when traditional bioburden tests won't work, but it must be clearly understood and carefully implemented.

Middle-aged people with high levels of a hormone called cortisol in their blood, because of stress, have impaired memory when compared to those with average levels of the hormone, even before symptoms of memory loss started to show, according to a study recently published. – American Academy of Neurology (AAN), Neurology®

Researchers have trained a machine learning algorithm to identify and predict which genes make infectious bacteria resistant to antibiotics. The approach was successfully tested on strains of Mycobacterium tuberculosis—the bacteria that cause tuberculosis (TB). – University of California San Diego
Nature Communications

Electrical engineer Koichi Takaki has used nanosecond-long pulses of high-voltage electricity and discharge plasma -- like that found in lightning -- to promote the growth of fruits, vegetables and edible fungi, and to preserve the freshness. – AVS: Science and Technology of Materials, Interfaces, and Processing
AVS 65th International Symposium and Exhibition

Cancer researchers in a Georgetown University-led study observed that a protein they investigated for its possible role in cancer, turned out to be a powerful regulator of metabolism. – Georgetown Lombardi Comprehensive Cancer Center
Scientific Reports

A new study of measuring blood pressure at home in U.S. populations has found that the ideal level is 130 over 80 or lower. – UT Southwestern Medical Center, American Heart Association (AHA); American College of Cardiology (ACC)

Bijuva becomes the first FDA-approved hormone therapy for the treatment of hot flashes.

A company has launched the 'Relay robot,' a new fully autonomous service robot designed to optimize labor productivity in hospital lab environments.

Mathematics, Science & Artificial Intelligence (AI)

Currently, non-dairy dessert toppings, prepared with healthier unsaturated fats, cannot match the same foam structure and stability as those prepared with saturated fats, thus negatively impacting the function and sensory properties of toppings of cakes and desserts. Researchers are looking for new formulations and ingredients for whipped topping emulsions that allow for the preparation of stable toppings using healthier mono- and polyunsaturated fats.

Building with natural clay is being regarded as a great alternative in Europe, as constructions using local soil have one of the lowest negative impacts. However, this development is particularly hindered by the high water sensitivity of clay based materials. Hence, specialists are looking for chemical additives to be added to clay and sand dry mixtures that will, after mixing with water and natural drying and hardening, lead to a long-term water resistant material that can be used as a construction material.

SpaceX was very successful its first-ever rocket landing in California, after successfully delivering Argentina's SAOCOM-1A Earth-observation satellite to orbit. SpaceX has already pulled off more than two dozen first-stage landings during orbital liftoffs, with the boosters coming down on "drone ships" stationed in the Atlantic and Pacific oceans, and on terra firma at Cape Canaveral Air Force Station in Florida.

Optical frequency combs can enable ultrafast processes in physics, biology, and chemistry, as well as improve communication and navigation, medical testing, and security. Columbia Engineers have built the smallest integrated Kerr frequency comb generator.
– Columbia University School of Engineering and Applied Science Nature Oct 8 2018

A report from Ernst and Young shows that artificial intelligence is not only helping now and for the foreseeable future, but that it's also going to have a much stronger presence in medtech as time goes on.

The world's first blockchain based phone, called the "XPhone", appears and claims to let you call, send messages, and transfer files, all by using blockchain instead of traditional carriers. The innovation aims to expand the use of blockchain technology beyond financial transfers. XPhone features include: A mobile Operating System built on the blockchain Sending and sharing data, such as SMS, securely via Function X blockchain. The XPhone OS is currently available to phone manufacturers for testing.

Reservoir sedimentation has become a significant problem with the aging of water storage facilities. Sediment deposition in reservoirs limits the active life of reservoirs by reducing storage capacity for water supply or flood risk reduction. Sedimentation also impacts dam outlets, reservoir water intakes, water quality, recreation, upstream flood stage, and downstream habitat. Researchers are working on sediment removal techniques for reservoir sustainability.

Specialists are looking how to improve the performance of marine lubricant formulations that use group base oils.

Starting as early as January 2017, the staff of a secret Facebook initiative called Building 8 have been working to make the world's first brain-computer interface, Business Insider reports. The initiative includes at least two major publicly reported projects: a noninvasive brain sensor designed to turn thoughts into text, and a device that essentially lets you "hear" with your skin.

To forge nanodiamonds, which have potential applications in medicine, optoelectronics and quantum computing, researchers expose organic explosive molecules to powerful detonations in a controlled environment. A new mathematical model helps define optimal temperature and pressure to forge nanoscale diamonds in an explosion. – American Institute of Physics (AIP)

The Journal of Chemical Physics

Researchers work on ideas for a system that can rapidly, accurately, and automatically delineate agricultural field outlines from multiple satellite imagery sources every year, storing the results in an efficient data structure for year to year comparison, and aggregation into common land units (CLU). The system should be applicable to large homogenous fields typical of the Midwestern United States, as well as heterogeneous fields typically found in sub-Saharan Africa.

Either exceedingly expensive fuel or very hot temperatures have made fuel cells a boutique proposition, but now there's one that runs on cheap methane, and at much lower temperatures. This is a practical, affordable fuel cell. – Georgia Institute of Technology
Nature Energy;

Researchers at Lawrence Berkeley National Laboratory and the Joint Center for Artificial Photosynthesis have developed an artificial photosynthesis device called a "hybrid photoelectrochemical and voltaic cell" that turns sunlight and water into electricity. – Nature Materials

General news and issues

Reports: Amazon has announced the minimum wage for its U.S. employees will be $15/hour, with the increase set to take effect next month. "We listened to our critics, thought hard about what we wanted to do, and decided we want to lead," said CEO Jeff Bezos. The move will benefit more than 350 K workers, including full-time, part-time, temporary and seasonal positions.

Reports: Some specialists say that Google has a tendency towards privatized authoritarianism.

Earlier this year, Branson admitted Virgin Galactic was in a closely-fought commercial space race with Jeff Bezos's Blue Origin.

The rapid escalation of Hurricane Oct-9-2018 in the Gulf of Mexico, which is forecast to become a major hurricane by 9 October 2018 evening, and make landfall on Wednesday, 10 Oct. The National Hurricane Center warning cone currently includes Florida, Alabama, Georgia, South Carolina, North Carolina, Virginia, Maryland, New Jersey and Delaware.
People ask for long time to name hurricanes with dates, not people's name, which is very insulting.

"We are starting to bump up against the absolute true fact that Earth is finite," Blue Origin founder Jeff Bezos declared, predicting there will be 1 T humans in the solar system one day. "The dynamism that I have seen over the last 20 years in the internet, where incredible things have happened in really short periods of time... We need thousands of companies." Blue Origin is "the most important thing" that Bezos is working on, he said, edging out Amazon and the Washington Post.

Reports: Many people are impressed how Amazon advanced from $5 per share in 1997 to more than $1,800 today, becoming America's second largest employer behind Walmart.

Reports: Amazon is opening its first office in Manchester, UK, and will hire more than 1,000 new staffers to work on R&D in the U.K. The new engineers will further develop personalized shopping recommendations, machine learning, Alexa, AWS and Amazon's drone delivery project Prime Air.

All people should understand that we all will live on the same planet Earth, which has certain planetary resources, and we will be much better if we will focus not only on growth in general, but on maximizing human well-being.

Reports: Research shows that those who are pet friendly, are people unfriendly.

Reports: Many Walmart customers are not happy with its Protection Plans, powered by Allstate – they send a very long e-mail, without any useful information – not even the name of the product, for which customers paid the protection, is not mentioned!

Reports: Research shows that ugly staff, like Halloween, is bad for your health, and especially for the mental health of children.

The Seattle, WA-based company Amazon, which wants to move in medical technology (an important decision!), is following a similar pattern to Google's Verily, when it comes down to making an impact in the healthcare industry.

Walmart-owned Sam's Club will soon open a cashier-free store concept that rivals Amazon Go.

31 October is World Savings Day – what nice it would be for the U.S to have $21.5 T in surplus, as savings, instead of deficit! Happy World Savings Day!

Amazon acquired online pharmacy startup PillPack, which is seen as a major move for the industry, as the e-commerce giant heads into the prescription drug business.

Humor

In a very modest house, a young wife jumps to her husband:
- Look there – a fly is on the wall!
    The husband looks at her:
- And what would you want – a Rembrandt!?

Finland, Helsinki: The Ateneum (1887). Center busts: Rafael, Phidias, and Bramante. Right: Benvenutto Cellini, Tessin. Left: Michelangelo, Rubens, Thorwaldsen, Rembrandt, Toesergel.

Universe Axioms

Formulated by Michael M. Dediu

The following axioms are not independent of each other. They express in different ways the same concept of infinity.

Axiom 1. Pointing a theoretical laser from Earth, in any direction, at any time, after a finite amount of time the laser beam will touch an astronomic body.

Axiom 2. In any direction in space starting from Earth, at any time, there is an astronomic body from which the Earth can be theoretically seen.

Axiom 3. Infinity of space: Any straight line passing through the Earth's center intersects an infinite number of astronomic bodies.

Axiom 4. Infinity of time: Representing the time on a line, with the origin at the beginning of the year 1, the time goes to infinite in both positive and negative directions.

Axiom 5. Infinity of life: Because of the infinity of space and time, it is normal to consider that the life exists at any time, in an infinite number of places. Therefore right now, when you are reading this book, there is life outside the Earth, in an infinite number of places, but we do not know yet how to contact them.

Axiom 6. The Earth rotates itself around its polar axis, the Moon and many artificial satellites rotate around the Earth, in the Solar System all the planets and many other objects rotate around the Sun, the Solar System itself rotates around the center of the Milky Way galaxy, the Milky Way galaxy and all the billions of galaxies in our

Universe (denoted U_1) rotate around the center of our Universe U_1, our Universe U_1, together with billions of other similar Universes, are inside a bigger Universe U_2 and rotate around the center of U_2, then U_2 and many others like it are inside a bigger U_3 and rotate around the center of U_3, and so on. Therefore, in general, the Universe U_n together with many similar Universes are inside the bigger Universe U_{n+1} and rotate around the center of U_{n+1}, for any n natural number, which goes to infinity. This can be written in the formula:

$$U_1 \subset U_2 \subset U_3 \subset \ldots \subset U_n \subset U_{n+1} \subset \ldots, \text{ n natural number.}$$

UK, Oxford, Oriel College (1326, in the east range of First quadrangle, the ornate portico in the center, with the inscription Regnante Carolo).

Time Axioms

Formulated by Michael M. Dediu

Axiom 1. Time is the most important force in the Univers.

Axiom 2. Everything is a function of time.

Axiom 3. Time exists in absolutely everything.

Axiom 4. Time creates and distroys everything.

Axiom 5. Time is invisible, inodor, insipid, unpalpabil, unaudible, but exists evrywhere.

Axiom 6. There are infinitezimal time particles, without mass, which are present everywhere, and which actually continuously transform everything.

UK, Cambridge, From Trinity Lane looking south to the west part of the northern façade and entrance of King's College Chapel (1446).

Bibliography

"The Histories" by Polybius
"Discours de la Méthode" by René Descartes
"Meditationes de prima philosophia" by René Descartes
"Philosophiae Naturalis Principia Mathematica" by Isaac Newton
Chinese encyclopedia Gujin Tushu Jicheng (Imperial Encyclopedia)
"Encyclopédie" by Jean-Baptiste le Rond d'Alembert and Denis Diderot
"Encyclopaedia Britannica" by over 4,400 contributors
"Encyclopedia Americana" by Francis Lieber

Michael M. Dediu is also the author of these books (which can be found on Amazon.com, and www.derc.com):

1. Aphorisms and quotations – with examples and explanations
2. Axioms, aphorisms and quotations – with examples and explanations
3. 100 Great Personalities and their Quotations
4. Professor Petre P. Teodorescu – A Great Mathematician and Engineer
5. Professor Ioan Goia – A Dedicated Engineering Professor
6. Venice (Venezia) – a new perspective. A short presentation with photographs
7. La Serenissima (Venice) - a new photographic perspective. A short presentation with many photos
8. Grand Canal – Venice. A new photographic viewpoint. A short presentation with many photos
9. Piazza San Marco – Venice. A different photographic view. A short presentation with many photos
10. Roma (Rome) - La Città Eterna. A new photographic view. A short presentation with many photos
11. Why is Rome so Fascinating? A short presentation with many photos
12. Rome, Boston and Helsinki. A short photographic presentation
13. Rome and Tokyo – two captivating cities. A short photographic presentation
14. Beautiful Places on Earth – A new photographic presentation

15. From Niagara Falls to Mount Fuji via Rome - A novel photographic presentation

16. From the USA and Canada to Italy and Japan - A fresh photographic presentation

17. Paris – Why So Many Call This City Mon Amour - A lovely photographic presentation

18. The City of Light – Paris (La Ville-Lumière) - A kaleidoscopic photographic presentation

19. Paris (Lutetia Parisiorum) – the romance capital of the world - A kaleidoscopic photographic view

20. Paris and Tokyo – a joyful photographic presentation. With a preamble about the Universe

21. From USA to Japan via Canada – A cheerful photographic documentary

22. 200 Wonderful Places, In The Last 50 Years – A personal photographic documentary

23. Must see places in USA and Japan - A kaleidoscopic photographic documentary

24. Grandeurs of the World - A kaleidoscopic photographic documentary

25. Corneliu Leu – writer on the same wavelength as Mark Twain. An American viewpoint

26. From Berkeley to Pompeii via Rome – A kaleidoscopic photographic documentary

27. From America to Europe via Japan - A kaleidoscopic photographic documentary

28. Discover America and Japan - A photographic documentary

29. J. R. Lucas – philosopher on a creative parallel with Plato, An American viewpoint

30. From America to Switzerland via France - A photographic documentary

31. From Bretton Woods to New York via Cape Cod - A photographic documentary

32. Splendid Places on the Atlantic Coast of the U. S. A. - A photographic documentary

33. Fourteen nice Cities on three Continents - A photographic documentary

34. 17 Picturesque Cities on the World Map - A photographic documentary

35. Unforgettable Places from Four Continents, including Trump buildings - A photographic documentary

36. Dediu Newsletter, Volume 1, Number 1, 6 December 2016 – Monthly news, review, comments and suggestions for a better and wiser world

37. Dediu Newsletter, Volume 1, Number 2, 6 January 2017 (available also at www.derc.com).

38. Dediu Newsletter, Volume 1, Number 3, 6 February 2017 (available at www.derc.com).

39. London and Greenwich, - A photographic documentary

40. Dediu Newsletter, Volume 1, Number 4, 6 March 2017 (available also at www.derc.com).

41. Dediu Newsletter, Volume 1, Number 5, 6 April 2017 (available also at www.derc.com).

42. Dediu Newsletter, Volume 1, Number 6, 6 May 2017 (available also at www.derc.com).

43. Dediu Newsletter, Volume 1, Number 7, 6 June 2017 (available also at www.derc.com).

44. London, Oxford and Cambridge, A photographic documentary

45. Dediu Newsletter, Volume 1, Number 8, 6 July 2017 (available also at www.derc.com).

46. Dediu Newsletter, Volume 1, Number 9, 6 August 2017 (available also at www.derc.com).

47. Dediu Newsletter, Volume 1, Number 10, 6 September 2017 (available also at www.derc.com).

48. Three Great Professors: President Woodrow Wilson, Historian German Arciniegas, and Mathematician Gheorghe Vranceanu – A chronological and photographic documentary

49. Dediu Newsletter, Volume 1, Number 11, 6 October 2017 (available also at www.derc.com).

50. Dediu Newsletter, Volume 1, Number 12, 6 November 2017 (available also at www.derc.com).

51. Dediu Newsletter, Volume 2, Number 1 (13), 6 December 2017 (available also at www.derc.com).

52. Two Great Leaders: Augustus and George Washington - A chronological and photographic documentary

53. Dediu Newsletter, Volume 2, Number 2 (14), 6 January 2018 (available also at www.derc.com).

54. Newton, Benjamin Franklin, and Gauss, A chronological and photographic documentary

55. Dediu Newsletter, Volume 2, Number 3 (15), 6 February 2018 (available also at www.derc.com).

56. 2017: World Top Events, But Many Little Known, A chronological and photographic documentary

57. Dediu Newsletter, Volume 2, Number 4 (16), 6 March 2018 (available also at www.derc.com).

58. Vergilius, Horatius, Ovidius, and Shakespeare - A chronological and photographic documentary.

59. Dediu Newsletter, Volume 2, Number 5 (17), 6 April 2018 (available also at www.derc.com).

60. Dediu Newsletter, Volume 2, Number 6 (18), 6 May 2018 (available also at www.derc.com).

61. Vivaldi, Bach, Mozart, and Verdi - A chronological and photographic documentary.

62. Dediu Newsletter, Volume 2, Number 7 (19), 6 June 2018 (available also at www.derc.com).

63. Dediu Newsletter, Volume 2, Number 8 (20), 6 July 2018 (available also at www.derc.com).

64. Dediu Newsletter, Volume 2, Number 9 (21), 6 August 2018 (available also at www.derc.com).

65. World History, a new perspective - A chronological and photographic documentary.

66. World Humor History with over 100 Jokes, a new perspective - A chronological and photographic documentary

67. Dediu Newsletter, Volume 2, Number 10 (22), 6 September 2018 (available also at www.derc.com).

68. Dediu Newsletter, Volume 2, Number 11 (23), 6 October 2018 (available also at www.derc.com).

Mathematical research papers published in international mathematical journals

1. Dediu, M. On the lens spaces. *Rev. Roumaine Math. Pures Appl*. **14** (1969) 623-627.

2. Dediu, M. Sur quelques propriétés des espaces lenticulaires. (French) *Rev. Roumaine Math. Pures Appl.* **17** (1972), 871-874.

3. Vranceanu, G; Dediu, M. Tangent vector fields in projective spaces V$_3$ and in the lens spaces L^3(3). (Romanian) Stud. Cerc. Mat. **24** (1972), 1585-1600.

4. Dediu, M. Tangent vector fields on lens spaces of dimension three (Italian) *Atti Accad. Naz. Lincei Rend. Cl. Sci. Fis. Mat. Natur.* **54** (1974), no. 2, 329-334 (1977

5. Dediu, M. Campi di vettori tangenti sullo spazio lenticolare L^7(3). (Italian) *Atti Accad. Naz. Lincei Rend. Cl. Sci. Fis. Mat. Natur. (8)* **58** (1975), no. 1, 14-17.

6. Dediu, M. Tre campi di vettori tangenti indepedenti sugli spazi lenticolari di dimensione 4n+3. (Italian) *Atti Accad. Naz. Lincei Rend. Cl. Sci. Fis. Mat. Natur. (8)* **58** (1975), no. 2, 174-178.

7. Dediu, M. Sopra la metrica Vranceanu generalizzata (Italian) *Atti Accad. Naz. Lincei Rend. Cl. Sci. Fis. Mat. Natur. (8)* **58** (1975), no.3, 354-359).

8. Dediu, M. Sopra la metrica Vranceanu generalizzata (Italian) *Atti Accad. Naz. Lincei Rend. Cl. Sci. Fis. Mat. Natur. (8)* **58** (1975), no.3, 354-359).

9. Dediu, S.; Dediu, M. Sopra gli spazi proiettivi. *Rend. Sem. Fac. Sci. Univ. Cagliari* **46** (1976), suppl., 149-152.

10. Dediu, M.; Caddeo, Renzo; Dediu Sofia Alcune proprietà di una superficie immersa in uno spazio di Hilbert. (Italian) *Rend. Ist. Mat. Univ. Trieste* **8** (1976), no. 2, 147-161 (1977)

11. Dediu, S.; Dediu, M.; Caddeo, R. Alcune proprietà della metrica di Vranceanu generalizzata. (Italian) *Rend Sem. Fac. Sci. Univ Cagliari* **46** (1976), suppl., 153-161.

12. Dediu, Sofia; Dediu, M.; Caddeo, Renzo The Vrănceanu metric in local coordinates. (Italian) *Atti Accad. Sci. Lett. Arti Palermo Parte I (4)* **37** (1977/78). 331-339 (1980)

13. Dediu, M.; Caddeo, Renzo; Dediu, Sofia The extension of an *E*-premanifold to an *E*-manifold. (Italian) *Rend. Circ. Mat. Palermo (2)* **27** (1978), no. 3, 353-358.

Japan: the northern side of Kawaguchiko (Lake Kawaguchi, 6 km², 830 m elevation), with a splendid statue (left), 17 km north of Mt. Fuji (3,776 m, 1707 last eruption), 100 km south-west of Tokyo.

Michael M. Dediu is the editor of these books (also on Amazon.com, and www.derc.com):

1. Sophia Dediu: The life and its torrents – Ana. In Europe around 1920
2. Proceedings of the 4th International Conference "Advanced Composite Materials Engineering" COMAT 2012
3. Adolf Shvedchikov: I am an eternal child of spring – poems in English, Italian, French, German, Spanish and Russian
4. Adolf Shvedchikov: Life's Enigma – poems in English, Italian and Russian
5. Adolf Shvedchikov: Everyone wants to be HAPPY – poems in English, Spanish and Russian
6. Adolf Shvedchikov: My Life, My Love – poems in English, Italian and Russian
7. Adolf Shvedchikov: I am the gardener of love – poems in English and Russian
8. Adolf Shvedchikov: Amaretta di Saronno – poems in English and Russian
9. Adolf Shvedchikov: A Russian Rediscovers America
10. Adolf Shvedchikov: Parade of Life - poems in English and Russian
11. Adolf Shvedchikov: Overcoming Sorrow - poems in English and Russian
12. Sophia Dediu: Sophia meets Japan
13. Corneliu Leu: Roosevelt, Churchill, Stalin and Hitler: Their surprising role in Eastern Europe in 1944
14. Proceedings of the 5th International Conference "Computational Mechanics and Virtual Engineering" COMEC 2013
15. Georgeta Simion – Potanga: Beyond Imagination: A Thought-provoking novel inspired from mid-20th century events
16. Ana Dediu: The poetry of my life in Europe and The USA
17. Ana Dediu: The Four Graces
18. Proceedings of the 5th International Conference "Advanced Composite Materials Engineering" COMAT 2014
19. Sophia Dediu: Chocolate Cook Book: Is there such a thing as too much chocolate?

20. Sorin Vlase: Mechanical Identifiability in Automotive Engineering
21. Gabriel Dima: The Evolution of the Aerostructures – Concept and Technologies
22. Proceedings of the 6th International Conference "Computational Mechanics and Virtual Engineering" COMEC 2015
23. Sophia Dediu: Cook Book 1 A-B-C Common sense cooking
24. Sophia Dediu: Dim Sum Spring Festival
25. Ana Dediu and Sophia Dediu: Europe in 1985: A chronological and photographic documentary

Italy, Rome (753 BC): the front of the Altare della Patria (1925), with an equestrian statue of Vittorio Emanuele II, 1820-1878.